COMMUNITY HELPERS

TEACHERS

Written by Eliza Nodes

Genius Kid

sales@northstareditions.com | 888-417-0195

Library of Congress Control Number:
The Library of Congress Control Number is available on the Library of Congress website.

ISBN
979-8-89471-053-2 (library bound)
979-8-89471-073-0 (paperback)
979-8-89471-112-6 (epub)
979-8-89471-093-8 (hosted ebook)

Printed in the United States of America
Mankato, MN
012026

Written by:
Eliza Nodes

Edited by:
Rebecca Phillips-Bartlett

Designed by:
Ker Ker Lee

All facts, statistics, web addresses, and URLs in this book were verified as valid and accurate at time of writing. No responsibility for any changes to external websites or references can be accepted by either the author or publisher.

Photo Credits – Images courtesy of Shutterstock.com, unless otherwise stated.

Cover – leungchopan, 19 STUDIO, Vera Aksionava, New Africa, lera lysenko, ASDF_MEDIA, SrideeStudio, Poznyakov, aldorado, SvetikovaV, Ljupco Smokovski, New Africa. 2–3 – Djomas, Rido. 4–5 – val lawless, Master of Stocks. 6–7 – OSTILL is Franck Camhi, wavebreakmedia, Creativa Images, JohnnyGreigiStockphoto. 8–9 – Ljupco Smokovski, Drazen Zigic, Monkey Business Images, Blaj Gabriel. 10–11 – Daisy Daisy, liyuhan, SGr, Robert Kneschkel. 12–13 – Ivana Perosevic, Serhii_Tesliuk_Tesla, fizkes, michaeljung. 14–15 – Pixel-Shot, stuar, Olga Kovalenko, RTimages. 16–17 – Krikkiat, Rept0n1x, Hugo Robledo, XanderSt, Stastny_Pavel, fast-stock, panitanphoto. 18–19 –Syda Productions, Roman Samborskyi. 20–21 – A Lot Of People, Ixepop, Djomas, Paisatges Verticals. 22–23 – Roman Samborskyi, ViDI Studio, New Africa, Ljupco Smokovski.

CONTENTS

Words that look like <u>this</u> can be found in the glossary on page 24.

TEACHERS

What do you think teachers do when they aren't teaching lessons?

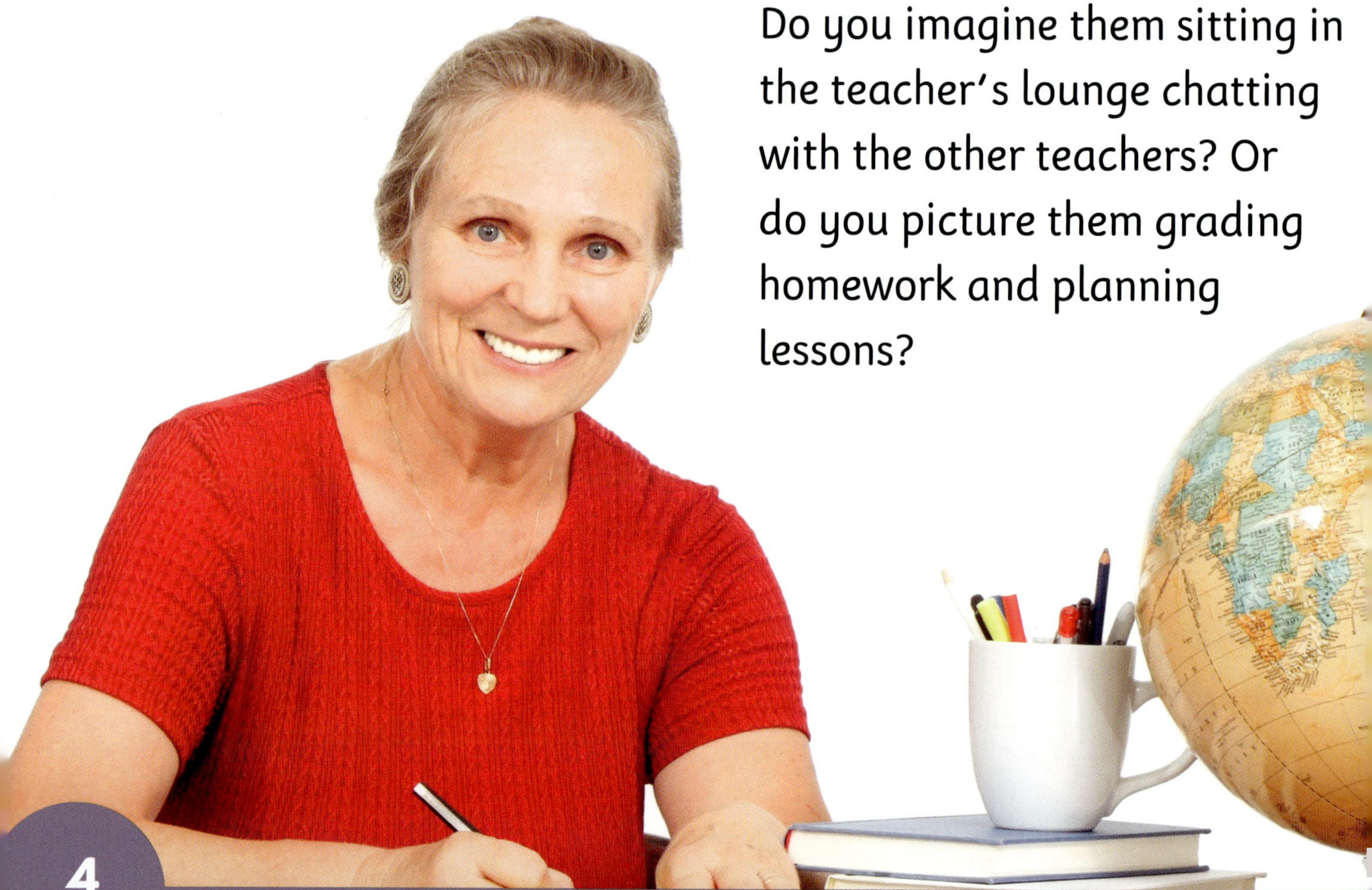

Do you imagine them sitting in the teacher's lounge chatting with the other teachers? Or do you picture them grading homework and planning lessons?

Teachers are important members of the community.
Some teachers work with children. Others work with adults.

Teachers look out for and protect the well-being of their students.

DID YOU KNOW?
Well-being is the state of being healthy and happy.

MANY JOBS IN ONE

A teacher's job involves many different tasks.

PLANNING LESSONS

Teachers follow lesson plans. They make sure they teach students everything the students need to know.

TEACHING LESSONS

Teachers explain different subjects such as math or reading.

SUPERVISING

Teachers supervise students at lunch and recess. They make sure students stay safe.

DECORATING THE CLASSROOM

Teachers decorate their classrooms. They use students' work or educational posters. Decorations make classrooms fun and safe places to learn.

MEETING WITH TEACHERS

A staff meeting is when teachers meet with the principals and other teachers. They discuss any problems or new ideas they have.

MEETING WITH PARENTS

Teachers meet with parents. They talk to parents about their child's progress. They may also talk about the student's behavior at school.

GRADING HOMEWORK

Teachers grade tests and homework. They may do this at school or take the work home.

LOOKING OUT FOR OTHERS

Teachers want to help their students. They may talk to students about any problems the students are facing.

AT THE SCHOOL

Schools have many different rooms.

CLASSROOMS

Classes take place in classrooms. Classrooms often have desks and whiteboards.

ATHLETIC FIELD

After-school sports and gym classes may take place on the athletic field. Sometimes recess takes place here, too.

GYM

Gym classes can take place inside the gym, too. Teachers might also use the gym to teach drama class or stage performances.

CAFETERIA

Students and some teachers eat lunch in the cafeteria. Teachers take turns supervising the students during lunch.

MUSIC ROOM

The music room is where music classes take place. After-school clubs such as band or choir may also use the music room to practice in.

LIBRARY

The library is full of books for students to read. Teachers might use the library for story time or checking out books.

COMPUTER ROOM

Computers are stored in the computer room. Students use the computers to learn skills such as research and typing.

TEACHER'S LOUNGE

The teacher's lounge is a room in the school just for the teachers. Teachers may chat, work, or discuss lessons. Some spend their lunchtime here.

EQUIPMENT

Every classroom needs equipment for students and teachers.

Students need to sit on chairs and at desks.

They need pens and pencils to write with. They need notebooks or paper to write on.

Many classrooms have interactive whiteboards. Teachers use interactive whiteboards to show images and videos to the whole class.

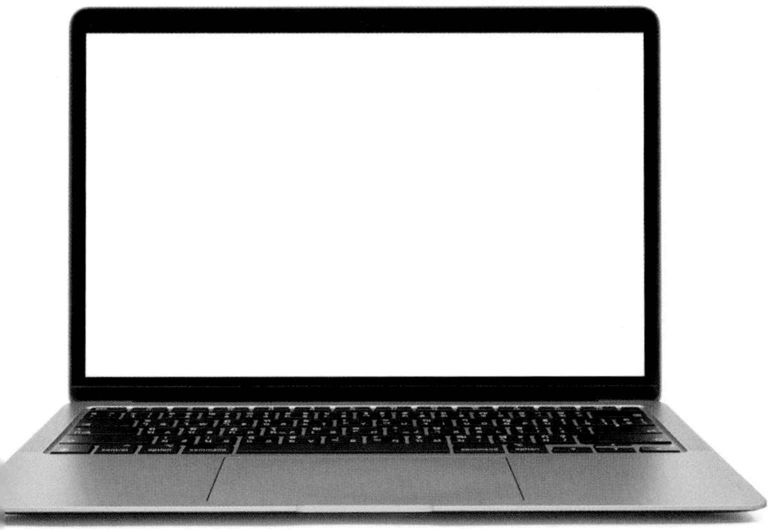

Many teachers have school laptops. Teachers use them to teach and do their work. This includes writing lesson plans and grading homework.

A HISTORY OF TEACHING

Ancient Greece
Tutors and school were mainly for wealthy males. However, in some parts of Greece, girls were allowed an education.

The 1800s
Women started to become teachers in the United States. Soon there were more female teachers than male teachers.

The 1600s
The first schools for girls opened in Europe. Only girls from rich families could afford to go.

The 1800s to the Late 1900s

Chalkboards were a common piece of equipment in classrooms.

The 1980s

Schools started to get computers. Computer lessons taught children how to use computers.

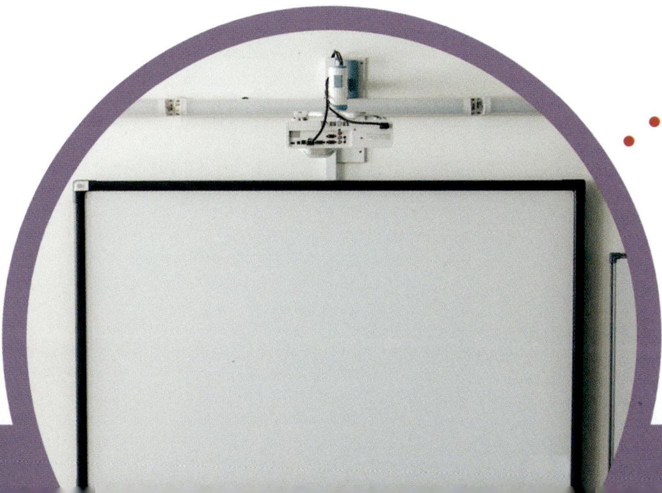

The 1990s

Interactive whiteboards started to be used in schools.

BECOMING A TEACHER

Teachers need a college degree. Then they decide what age they want to focus on. Some teachers teach young kids. Others work at colleges.

DID YOU KNOW?
Some teachers teach all subjects to one age group. Others teach one subject to many age groups.

It's important for teachers to love the subject they teach. The more they care about it, the more their students will be interested in it.

Teachers need to be patient. They need to remain calm in stressful situations.

BELIEVE IT OR NOT!

There are more than 90 million teachers around the world.

Most teachers are called by their last names. In other countries, such as Finland, students call their teachers their first names. What do you call your teacher?

Most teachers in the world are women.

In the 1800s, schoolchildren wrote their work with chalk on pieces of rock called slate. Pens, ink, and paper were too expensive for schools to buy at the time.

ARE YOU A GENIUS KID?

Now you know many things about teachers. Your friends and family are going to be so amazed by all your facts! How much can you remember? Let's do a quiz to find out.

Check back through the book if you are not sure.

1. True or False: Teachers need a college degree.
2. Name two tasks that are part of a teacher's job.
3. When did schools start getting computers?

Answers:
1. True, 2. Planning lessons; teaching lessons; supervising; decorating the classroom; meeting with teachers; meeting with parents; grading homework; or looking out for others, 3. The 1980s.

GLOSSARY

community a group of people who are connected by something

decorate to add something to an object or room in order to make it look better

equipment items that are needed to complete a certain job

interactive two-way communication between a computer and a person

supervise to watch over

tutors people who privately teach one or a few students

INDEX